MW00887842

HOP Beginners Guide To Doing Safety Differently

Controls Save Lives - The 6th Principle of HOP?

By Brent Sutton and Jeffery Lyth, and foreword by Todd Conklin. Contributions from Josh Bryant.

© Learning Teams Inc 2024

Published: September 2024
ISBN: 979-8327264915

PROLOGUE

I am often asked, "Why do Jenga blocks appear in many HOP publications?".

The story is that the game Jenga ®[1] involves removing one block from a tower constructed of 54 blocks at a time. Each block removed is then placed on top of the tower, creating a progressively taller and unstable structure until someone's misstep (either on removing a block or on placing it unsteadily on top of the destabilizing structure) leads to it crashing down. This is the perfect analogy for the concepts of complexity in systems, as well as HOP (Human and Organizational Performance), which can be explored through several key perspectives:

■ **Fragility and Stability in Complex Systems:** A Jenga tower is a metaphor for complex systems, often composed of interconnected and interdependent elements. In Jenga, each block represents a component of the system. The tower's stability depends on each block's integrity and interaction. Similarly, removing or altering one element in complex systems can have unpredictable and potentially destabilizing effects on the entire system. This illustrates the fragile balance in complex organizations and ecosystems, where changes in one part can lead to significant and often unforeseen consequences in another.

---

[1] JENGA® is a registered trademark owned by Pokonobe Associates.

■ **Incremental Change and Risk Management:** In Jenga, players take turns removing one block at a time, akin to making incremental changes in a system or organization. This process requires careful risk assessment and an understanding of each move's implications. It mirrors the decision-making process in organizations where people must evaluate the impact of their actions, balancing innovation and progress against the potential risks of destabilizing the system.

■ **Adaptability and Learning:** As the game progresses, the structure becomes increasingly unstable, requiring players to adapt their strategies. This reflects the need for adaptability in complex systems and organizations. Organizations that can learn from their current environment and past events and adjust accordingly are more likely to succeed.

■ **Interconnectedness and Team Dynamics:** Jenga is often played in teams, highlighting the importance of collaboration, communication, cooperation, and understanding the interconnectedness of work in a group setting.

■ **Thresholds and Catastrophic Failure:** The collapse of a Jenga tower can be sudden and dramatic, illustrating the concept of thresholds in complex systems. Systems can absorb change up to a point, but a rapid and irreversible shift can lead to failure or collapse once a critical threshold is crossed. This concept is essential in understanding how systems can deteriorate or fail and the importance of recognizing and respecting limits in both natural and organizational environments.

- ■ **Predictability and Uncertainty:** While the basic rules of Jenga are simple, predicting the outcome of each move becomes increasingly difficult as the game progresses. This unpredictability mirrors the inherent uncertainty in complex systems, where, despite having rules and controls, the exact outcomes of interactions within the system can be challenging to predict.

- ■ **Feedback Loops:** The Jenga game demonstrates feedback loops, where each move affects the tower's stability and influences subsequent decisions. In complex systems, feedback loops play a crucial role, where the outcomes of actions can reinforce or undermine the system's stability.

The Jenga tower is a powerful metaphor for understanding the dynamics of complex systems, emphasizing the importance of balance, adaptability, risk assessment, and the interconnected nature of elements within a system. These concepts directly apply to the human performance of workers and the organization's performance, underscoring the need for awareness, adaptability, and learning of the broader impacts of system work design and conditions in complex environments.

HOP helps us make the system's complexity more visible or transparent and a way to support better work without too many "uh-oh, I messed up!" moments before the safety system collapses like a game of Jenga.

Brent Sutton

Other books in this series

Volume 1: Introduction to HOP

Volume 2: Human Error

Volume 3: Controls Save Lives - The 6th Principle of HOP

Volume 4: Learning and Caring From Events and Restorative Culture

Volume 5: Learning and Improving For Better Work

Volume 6: Introduction to Learning Teams

Volume 7: Asking Better Questions or Seeking Better Stories

Volume 8: Critical Risks, Critical Controls, and Critical Steps

Volume 9: Frontline Leadership

Volume 10: Applying HOP Beyond Safety: The Value of Operational Learning

Please note: This is subject to change.

FOREWORD BY TODD CONKLIN

So, you know that for years and years and years, we've had these five principles. And I'm not sure why we have five, except we have five.

The original principles that emerged from the INPO (Institute of Nuclear Power Operations) were five, and they made good sense. We used them for years, and Shane Bush and I taught them across the country and talked about them. You could hear Rob Fisher and Tony Muschara talking about them, and you could go to almost any facility in North America and hear about the five principles.

Those five principles are five principles. I never thought about why there are five or how come there's not 11, or how come there's not two; there's five. And we've talked about them on my Pre-Accident Investigation podcast a bunch; you know, people make mistakes, blame fixes nothing, learning is vital to operations, context drives behavior, and how leadership responds matters.

And those principles have, over time, morphed and grown and matured. And that's all been pretty normal. I mean, it's been 25-plus years on these five principles. They're gonna change. And we're learning more, and we're getting smarter.

And the world is much more complex, which seems impossible, but it totally is. And so now what's happening is there's been a relatively interesting discussion about adding a sixth principle. And the funny thing to me is that people say it to me as if it will be super controversial.

I don't know if I feel that way because I'm not sure if five is the right answer. I haven't thought about it. I do know that there's a principle and a practice, and principles guide practices. Therefore, principles are an important part of how we think as an organization.

Organizations need to have a set of core principles. That's really valuable. When I think of principles, I think of the organization as like a river. Your organization is constantly in motion. It's never the same twice. It's got interesting oddities, eddies, waterfalls and is affected by changing conditions, But riverbanks have guiding features that keep the river moving in some direction.

Principles are guiding things; they guide the organization's flow and direction. They help guide decisions, clarify, and understand the direction that the organization wants to move in. So that's a great thing.

So, the sixth principle this book discusses, "Controls Save Lives," is important for us to discuss. I love the idea of adding control saves lives; it increases its importance, it's clever, it's interesting, and it does tack on nicely as an additional sixth principle.

The other thing I should say is that I'm not convinced that the five principles are the only ones in the world and should never be touched. I don't think it's an inclusive representation of everything humankind knows.

But I believe there's a huge difference between a principle and a practice. So, a principle says people make mistakes, right? That's a principle. We understand that people will still make mistakes because people are fallible, and even your best people make mistakes.

For example, accountability is not a principle; it is a practice. One of the things that we struggle with in organizations throughout the globe is this idea of, well, how do I hold workers accountable? Yet, you don't hold workers accountable as an outcome because accountability is a practice. It's how you run your organization. And accountability is probably more important pre-event than it is in establishing post-event. But that's the practice idea.

I think this is a good conversation to have about "Controls Save Lives." It's necessary, and this discussion has merit. This book is a good idea because it facilitates this thinking.

"Controls save lives is something you do. It is a practice."

INTRODUCTION

WHY THE BOOK - BRENT SUTTON

In August 2023, I talked with Bobby Cowger about his HOP journey and what led him to his new podcast show, The HOPcast. I jokingly told Bobby that he was a HOP Millennial "HOPster," which I meant as a compliment. The conversation with Bobby made me think about how our workforce is changing, as the baby boomers and Gen X's make way for most of our workforce to Millennials and Gen Z. It made me think about how the HOP Principles and our emerging workforce align. I undertook some non-academic study into the topic and discovered that they;

- Want to have a say and contribute their ideas. They resist doing repetitive or tedious work. They desire to have a life outside of work and expect enough flexibility to allow them to fulfill both their personal and professional commitments.

- Want to be supported, receive feedback, be mentored, and feel appreciated. That doesn't make them dependent but quite strategic. They think about what they need to be successful, and that's what they ask for.

- Want work that enables them to contribute positively to society and appropriately rewards them. One isn't a substitute for the other.

- Are comfortable with technology but also believe that feeling like they have a community at work is a determining factor in organizational commitment, job satisfaction, engagement, and retention.

■ Are committed when they mostly get what they need; they don't want to leave; they want to move up in the organization. But being committed isn't blind loyalty or staying no matter what.

I concluded that the HOP Principles and the values of our new workforce are closely aligned. And if more people like Bobby spread the word about HOP and if we baby boomers and Gen X support and mentor them on their journey of learning and improving, then there will be a learning and improving future for all of us.

This was the impetus for this book series. A series of beginner guides that explored HOP, tools, and integration themes for everyone (not just Millennials).

A book series written by non-academics for non-academics. A book series that was not only relatable to people but also created a call to action, "HOP Into Action®," which is our safety differently approach to building human capability, capacity, and resilience in all things HOP, using a scaffolded learning approach, which we call CCR®[2] (Capability, Capacity, and Resilience).

This book series has been designed to support this. We will help you to improve your;

■ **Capability** of HOP knowledge and understanding through this body of knowledge and stories from real people.

■ **Capacity** to go out into the real world and use the activities in the book to try out the concepts, themes, tools, and approaches to create the link between learning and improving.

---

[2] CCR (Capability, Capacity and Resilience) and HOP Into Action are trademarks for Learning Teams Inc.

■ **Resilience** as you learn, reflect, and adapt to the challenges you will encounter on your journey, using the learning, reflection, and coaching journal in each book.

We want you to start where you have experience so you can evaluate and assess the gap between where you are now and where you need to be. It is not about perfection; like all journeys, there will be bumps, and there need to be bumps. We learn from these bumps, and we improve from these bumps if we reflect.

Remember, look for the little wins; it is about winning the battle, not the war.

In closing, as a proud New Zealander, I leave you with these wise words from New Zealand explorer Sir Edmund Hillary, who was the first climber to reach the summit of Mt Everest in 1953.

It is not the mountain we conquer but ourselves.

You don't have to be a fantastic hero to do certain things -to compete.

You can be just an ordinary person, sufficiently motivated to reach challenging goals.

WHY THE BOOK - JEFFERY LYTH

I suggested that we write "The 6th Principle of HOP: Controls Save Lives" volume because I believe that something crucial was being overlooked in the way people practice Human and Organizational Performance (HOP).

Todd Conklin once spoke about the "5 principles 'plus one'," and this concept has stuck with me over the years. My work in fatality investigations has consistently shown that it is ultimately uncontrolled energy that kills people.

This realization, coupled with the concern that the foundational importance of high-order controls might be missed by those newly practicing HOP principles, led us to write this volume of the series.

Many companies have begun to internalize the HOP principles into their documents and programs, often adding the principle "controls save lives" or "safeguards save lives". I noticed this trend and felt that it was time to delve deeper into the concept and explore it more thoroughly and share those learnings with the wider community.

In Conklin's "5 Principles of Human Performance," he suggests that readers should be familiar with the foundational work that preceded what is now known as HOP. Unfortunately, this important step seems to be overlooked by many.

The original practices from the Institute of Nuclear Power Operations (INPO) and the Human Performance tools and concepts developed by the U.S. Department of Energy (DOE) in their Human Performance manuals laid the groundwork for what HOP has become.

This book is an effort to bring that foundational knowledge back to the forefront in applied HOP and emphasize the critical role that high-order controls play in saving lives.

HOP principles are a desire to improve safety and reliability in organizations and a shift in thinking about how people behave and organizations function

HOP PRINCIPLES RECAP

The five principles of HOP (in order of sense-making) are:

- **Error Is Normal; People Make Mistakes**: This principle acknowledges that errors are a normal part of human behavior and should be expected. The focus should not be on the error itself but on creating systems that tolerate inevitable errors.

- **Context Drives Behavior**: The conditions under which work is conducted greatly influence worker behavior. Good systems and processes help manage the uncertain operational outcomes that are always present in organizations.

- **Blame Fixes Nothing**: Blaming individuals for mistakes does not improve operational efficiency. Instead, it discourages the disclosure of important operational data and hinders learning and improvement.

- **How You Respond to Failure Matters**: Leaders can choose to use failures as opportunities for learning and improvement, or they can choose to punish those involved. The former approach encourages disclosure of information about failures and leads to organizational improvement, while the latter discourages such disclosure and hinders improvement.

- **Learning and Improving is Vital**: Organizations have two choices when responding to failure: to learn and improve or to blame and punish. Choosing to learn from failures is a strategic choice toward improvement.

However, try not to think of the HOP Principles as a list of commandments or an order in which they must be applied. The HOP Principles are more effective when working together as a mutual reliance (interdependent) instead of co-dependent on one another (meaning if one isn't present, the rest are ineffective).

We have used a "pictorial metaphor" of a pentagon to suggest the interdependent associations. For example, suppose a leader responds negatively to an event by blaming the actions of individuals. In that case, the ability for learning by the organization and the frontline workers will be reduced, and the broader system improvements may be limited by focusing on human error as the "cause and effect" of the event.

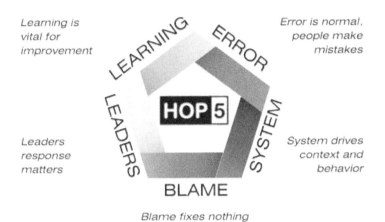

The HOP 5 Pentagon © Learning Teams Inc, 2024.

"Navigating high-risk work is a dance with uncertainty, where every step demands courage, precision, unwavering focus, and decision making amidst the unknown. Organizations give trust when work goes well, yet create distrust when work goes wrong" - Brent Sutton

CHAPTER ONE: HOP, CRITICAL RISKS AND CRITICAL CONTROLS

MANAGING RISK OR LEARNING AND IMPROVING UNCERTAINTY - BRENT SUTTON

The purpose of Risk Management is to assist organizations in integrating an effective decision-making framework into their governance, leadership, and culture.

Risks can include anything that generates uncertainty related to an organization's objectives or creates a deviation from the expected. This involves not only threats to the strength or viability of the organization but also opportunities to be gained.

In safety, we use lots of language with risk, including risk values, risk assessment, risk appetite, risk perception, etc. We perform risk assessments believing that it is about managing risk in the future, but in reality, the intent is to make it safer in the present because you can't predict the future (you can't predict something that hasn't happened yet). We want to believe that risk assessments are somehow scientific and that there must be a most accurate method to tell us what the answer is.

Typically you see two ways to look at risk within the context of safety, one is an engineering way to look at your systems and determine all their failure modes and effects, then you can tack on controls and understand risk by giving it some kind of value, usually based upon the frequency, the potential for the event happening, and in fact, the consequence if the event takes place.

So this is low potential, high consequence, high potential, low consequence, or anywhere in between there. We then use colours (green, amber, red), numbers and labels (low, medium, high) to describe and communicate risk.

The other is about human psychology, behavior, and all our biases. We have to understand every potential bias and human nuance to understand and even get close to being successful in understanding where risk is. This has particularly become prevalent around the discussions of psychosocial risks and psychological harm.

It can't be one or the other, the world is filled with lots of complexities and uncertainty (just reflect on the pandemic of 2020), therefore the answer lies somewhere in between, meaning you can't entirely focus on human behavior or you can't entirely focus on engineering. This is where the role of Human and Organizational Performance "HOP" Principles helps to bridge the divide.

I enjoy the work of Tony Muschara, who talks about the reality that

WORK = RISK

and that work is necessary to create value in the organization. Work requires people to touch, oversee, manipulate, record, or alter things. Jobs and tasks comprise a series of human actions designed to change material or information to create outputs.

Those things (hazards) that workers have to interact with or be close to having energy and harm occurs when that energy is released.

This notion of energy and harm was led in the 1970s by injury prevention scholar Dr. William Haddon. He pioneered the idea that every illness or injury results from unwanted contact with energy and that harm to the worker results when energy is transferred in quantities or at rates that the human body cannot withstand.

The energy wheel is the current reflection of this work and the system's ability to manage these energies and support workers in recognizing the presence of energy through hazard recognition.

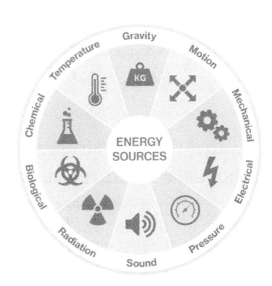

Therefore, the risk of harm emerges when people work because they are exposed to hazards, and those hazards have energy, which in turn creates risk.

And if the risk of harm from the hazard is life-changing or life-altering, we call them Critical Risks.

So here is the dilemma we are faced with:

IF WORK = RISK

AND IF WORK CAN'T BE FREE OF RISK - THEN WHAT?

AND IF RISK IS PRESENT - THEN THE POTENTIAL FOR HARM FROM ENERGY IS PRESENT?

AND IF THAT ENERGY IS NOT REMOVED OR REDUCED DURING WORK, IS IT A QUESTION OF **IF** OR **WHEN** AN EVENT CAN HAPPEN?

AND DOES THIS CONFLICT WITH THE NOTION OF ZERO HARM?

Because all work involves some level of risk, the system or people occasionally lose control of these hazards. That life-changing or life-altering event is when high amounts of energy is released and transferred to the worker(s) doing the work.

Human error is normal and a natural part of being human. It is not a problem until it occurs in synch with a hazard when energy can be released, and harm can occur.

Human performance is the greatest source of variation in any operation, and the uncertainty in this performance cannot be eliminated. Therefore, work involves risk under uncertain conditions.

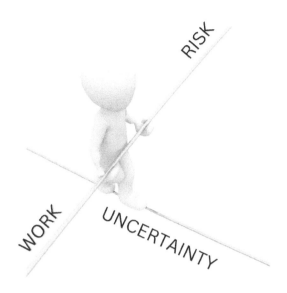

(c) Learning Teams Inc 2023

In a rules-based approach, human error is a cause.

In a systems-based approach, human error is a consequence.

In a learning-based approach, human error is a symptom of system complexity and uncertainty.

In the world of HOP, a system reduces the effect of uncertainty by allowing **workers to fail safely** (meaning that energy is prevented from being transferred to the worker) and/or the **system to fail gracefully** (meaning the amount of energy is reduced to minimize the impact of harm to the worker and property).

That system comprises barriers, defenses, controls, and mitigations - "safety measures" that should introduce certainty into work.

They are designed to directly manage the hazard from releasing energy or respond to, or recover from, the energy release.

There are also defenses, controls, and mitigations that attempt to influence how the worker performs the work.

Barriers, defenses, and controls are actions that reduce an event's probability of happening (prevention), whereas mitigation is an action that reduces the impact of the event.

The potential consequence/severity or impact of uncertainty from the "residual risk" is then transferred to workers to deal with, which happens in normal everyday work. In this situation, it is up to the organization to determine its appetite for risk.

You don't need a fancy label, number, or color to tell you that!

"We live in an ever-changing world where we are forced to deal with uncertainty every day. But how an organization tackles that uncertainty can be a key predictor of its success." ISO 31000:2018

THE HP AND HOP ORIGINS - JEFFERY LYTH

THE ORPHANED PRINCIPLE

In Volume One of the series, we explored the origins of HOP as a safety philosophy that emerged from the Nuclear Energy Sector in North America in the recognition that human error is normal and will happen and that systems should be designed to be more resilient to these errors.

And how the principles of HOP have been influenced by various sources, including the INPO/DOE (Institute of Nuclear Power Operations/ Department Of Energy) handbook, and continue to evolve. These HP (Human Performance) principles have been used to create a philosophical shift in thinking about how people behave in organizations and how organizations function best with the workers in the organization.

The original HP Principles from the INPO/DOE handbook were:

1. People are fallible, and even the best people make mistakes.

2. Error-likely situations are predictable, manageable, and preventable.

3. Individual behavior is influenced by organizational processes and values.

4. People achieve high levels of performance because of the encouragement and reinforcement received from leaders, peers, and subordinates.

5. Events can be avoided through an understanding of the reasons mistakes occur and the application of the lessons learned from past events (or errors).

The "Orphaned Principle" refers to the removal of a key idea from the original HP Principle 2. This idea was that we could predict, manage, and prevent situations where people are likely to make errors.

I suggest that Todd Conklin, who adapted these original principles into what is now known as HOP principles, may have left it out because it focused too much on 'fixing the human' and assumed that we could always foresee and prevent mistakes.

The original principle suggested that even though people make mistakes, certain mistakes could be predicted and avoided by recognizing risky situations. However, one could argue that this view is too simplistic, as it assumes we can completely predict and control human behavior in complex situations.

From the 'HOP' perspective, trying to predict and prevent all human errors isn't practical. Instead, we should accept that mistakes will happen and focus on designing systems that can handle these errors without causing serious problems. The idea is to improve the work environment so that even when mistakes occur, they don't lead to disasters. This approach shifts the focus from trying to control every error to making sure that when errors happen, they don't have catastrophic outcomes.

> The informal 6th HOP principle, "Controls Save Lives," highlights the importance of safety measures in protecting people and ensuring the smooth operation of systems in high-risk environments.

INTRODUCTION TO CRITICAL CONTROLS – BRENT SUTTON

If you have Critical Risks, then surely you need Critical Controls?

In complex systems and high-risk environments, controls act as vital safeguards, ensuring the integrity and resilience of workers performing their jobs and the organizational processes and assets.

This principle underscores the role of effective critical controls in;

- Mitigating organization risks (production, brand, etc)

- Improving operations (quality, safety, outcomes)

- Mitigating the safety risk of hazardous energy (STKY - Stuff That Can Kill You) physically, harm to health, and mental health.

- Improving methods of working, including how we work, the tools we use, how we communicate, and how we are empowered across physical harm, harm to health, and mental health perspectives.

So if we were to link the 6th HOP Principle - Controls Save Lives to this, then the key tenet to support this would be:

Proactive Risk Management: Critical Control Verification serves as a proactive measure to identify, assess, and mitigate the potential hazards of insufficient controls before they fail to prevent incidents or accidents.

By implementing a robust control validation program, organizations can anticipate and address vulnerabilities in their hazard identification, risk assessment, control systems, and critical control degradation, pre-empting adverse outcomes.

Redundancy and Back-Up Systems: Incorporating redundancy and back-up systems into operational processes enhances reliability and builds error-tolerant systems. These redundancies act as fail-safes, offering alternative pathways and mechanisms to maintain functionality even in the face of unexpected failures or disruptions.

Continuous Monitoring for Adaptation: Effective controls require continuous monitoring to maintain operational fidelity and adapt to evolving circumstances and environments. Organizations must remain vigilant, regularly verifying and validating that their control measures effectively address emerging risks and optimize performance.

Human-Centric Design: Controls should be designed with human capabilities and limitations in mind, supporting operators in executing tasks safely and efficiently. User-friendly interfaces, clear procedures, and ergonomic considerations are essential components of control systems that empower human performance.

Learning and Improvement: Control Validation is a valuable feedback mechanism, facilitating organizational learning and improvement. By analyzing the effectiveness of existing controls and learning from those who perform the work, organizations can refine their strategies, enhance their resilience, and continuously improve operational potential.

> Critical controls should not just manage threats; they should create opportunities for system and operational improvements and ways of doing better work. - Brent Sutton

WHAT IS THE JUSTIFICATION FOR THE 6TH PRINCIPLE - JEFFERY LYTH

Whether you believe this 6th Principle needs to be justified or not, there will be a need to be able to articulate the value in applying it in practice.

Here are six operational reasons to support this:

Emphasizing the Role of Controls in Managing Risk

In the HOP framework, the understanding is that human error is inevitable, but its consequences can be managed through effective controls. The principle "Controls Save Lives" aligns with this by focusing on the proactive identification and reinforcement of critical controls that prevent catastrophic failures. This principle would shift the safety focus from preventing all errors to ensuring that robust controls are in place to manage the high risk/high energy work when errors occur.

Acknowledging Human Variability

HOP teaches that human variability is not only expected but should be planned for within safety systems. The new principle emphasizes that systems should be designed with layers of controls that can absorb the variability in human performance. For instance, controls should be robust enough to handle situations where human performance might not be perfect. This includes designing systems where critical steps and the identification of risk-important actions by workers are supported by controls that do not rely solely on flawless human performance.

Focusing on Critical Controls and Critical Steps

The concept of critical controls and critical steps is central to managing high-risk tasks. By focusing on these elements, the new principle would guide organizations to identify and validate these controls rigorously.

For example, before performing any critical step, controls should be verified to ensure they are functioning correctly and can prevent or mitigate failure.

Preventing Over-Reliance on Human Performance

Another HOP tenet is that systems should not rely solely on human performance, especially in high-risk scenarios. "Controls Save Lives" would reinforce this by advocating for the use of automated or engineered controls wherever possible, thereby reducing the reliance on human action to maintain safety. This approach acknowledges that while humans are adaptable, they are also fallible, and systems should be designed to support them.

Encouraging a Shift from Blame to Learning

The new principle would also encourage a cultural shift from blaming individuals when controls fail to a focus on learning and improving the control mechanisms. This aligns with the HOP philosophy of treating humans as the solution rather than the problem, promoting continuous improvement in safety practices by learning from everyday work and incidents.

Practical Implementation and Verification

"Controls Save Lives" would call for regular verification of controls through practices like Critical Control Verification (CCV), ensuring that controls are not only present but also effective under the conditions in which they are needed. This proactive approach would help maintain a high level of safety by continuously assessing and enhancing the control environment.

WHY DO WE SEE HUMANS AS THE THREAT - BRENT SUTTON

In Volume 2 of this series titled "Human Error," we explored how human error could be viewed in two ways: the person approach and the system approach.

Each has its own model of error causation, and each model gives rise to different philosophies of error management. Understanding these differences has important practical implications for this 6th Principle of "Controls Save Lives."

It is a people problem: The long-standing and widespread tradition of the person approach focuses on the unsafe acts—errors and procedural violations—of people on the front line. It views these unsafe acts as arising primarily from aberrant mental processes such as forgetfulness, inattention, poor motivation, carelessness, negligence, and recklessness. The associated countermeasures are directed mainly at reducing unwanted variability in human behavior. These methods include poster campaigns that appeal to people's fear, writing another procedure (or adding to existing ones), disciplinary measures, threat of litigation, retraining, naming, blaming, and shaming. Followers of these approaches tend to treat errors as moral issues, assuming that bad things happen to bad people—what psychologists have called the "just-world hypothesis" in the belief that the world is fair and, consequently, that the moral standings of our actions will determine our outcomes.

It is a system problem: The basic premise in the system approach is that humans are fallible and errors are to be expected, even in the best organizations. Errors are seen as consequences rather than causes, having their origins not so much in the perversity of human nature as in "upstream" systemic factors. These include recurrent error traps in the workplace and the organizational processes that give rise to them. Countermeasures are based on the assumption that although we cannot change the human condition, we can change the conditions under which humans work. The central idea is that of system defenses. All hazardous technologies possess barriers and safeguards. When an adverse event occurs, the important issue is not who blundered but how and why the defenses failed.

This people versus system problem is also visible in our safety management system with policies and procedures. A leading academic in this space of Safety Science, Professor Erik Hollnagel said:

Safety can be a condition where the number of unacceptable outcomes is as low as possible, or

Safety is a condition where the number of acceptable outcomes is as high as possible.

This is what Professor Erik Hollnagel talks about the difference between "**Managing Safety**" versus "**Managing Safely**."

THE HOP LENS TO CRITICAL RISKS - BRENT SUTTON

The origins of HOP from the DOE (Department of Energy) Human Performance Handbooks provided a comprehensive framework for managing critical risks and controls within DOE nuclear facilities.

They emphasized a strategic approach to improving human performance and operations, focusing on three primary challenges:

■ **Understand Critical Activities/Tasks**: Identify and understand what tasks are critical to operational performance, environment, and safety.

■ **Error Management:** Strategies for anticipating (not predicting) the inevitability of human error, mitigating the impact, and identifying improvement potential through learning.

■ **Defense-in-Depth**: Layered controls to mitigate the impact of errors on people, infrastructure, and the environment. And an improved approach to enhance the integrity of controls. The concept of defense-in-depth involves multiple, overlapping controls to ensure redundancy. This approach ensures that if one control fails, others will still function to prevent or mitigate adverse events.

The DOE recognized the role of the organization, its leaders, and those who do the work and are exposed to risk in everyday work.

Organizational factors, including resource allocation, process execution, and adherence to high standards, are critical in managing controls. The document stresses that significant events often reflect organizational failures, and robust management practices that are workable, relatable, and available are essential for good operations.

Leadership practices, organizational culture, and systems of work influence how people perceive, think, and behave.

It is understood that the administrative element of safety, such as documented procedures, training, organizational policies, and rules to guide human actions, are less reliable due to their dependence on being able to influence the worker in a complex system.

By acknowledging that;

■ Systems are always degrading

■ Controls weaken over time, and

■ People are variable,

Continuous improvement is vital to address vulnerabilities and ensure that controls remain robust.

The HOP lens supports this notion of "Managing Safely" with the HOP Principles and language such as;

People can fail but fail safely.

The system can fail but fail gracefully.

Workers are only as safe as they need to be.

How people perform in the system is essential, and understanding performance modes helps us avoid "error-likely situations" and build better work; learning from why work goes well is more valuable than waiting to learn when work goes wrong.

We must have controls, barriers, and defenses (safeguards) in place for the inevitability of human error when work involves energy that can harm or kill us (STKY - S**t That Can Kill You).

Design and build better, more error-tolerant systems because systems and context drives behavior, and people will make mistakes.

Critical Risk Controls - A Magic Potion For Leaders - Todd Conklin

In a 2019 New Zealand Business Leaders Forum interview, Dr Todd Conklin discussed Critical Risk Controls. He stated that if he talked to a whole group of chief executives about safety and shook them up, he wouldn't talk to them about complacency. He would talk to them about controls. He guessed that for most chief executives, if nothing bad is happening, they assume that their risk is low.

In reality, what is probably truer is that if nothing bad happens, their risk doesn't change. It's not lower.

What changed is that their ability to control risk got better. And so, instead of being complacent to risk, he would talk to them about being sensitive to controls, to being really aware, to validate and verify the presence of the essential controls that need to be in work so that when the work fails, it fails gently, it fails successfully, it fails safely.

The very best thing a senior leader can do is become incredibly interested, not in how the organization failed to prevent the event but in how the organization failed to control it.

That difference, which may sound pretty nuanced, is huge. Because prevention is one-third of the safety picture, control is another full-third of the safety picture. And the absence of control is really frightening.

What scares him more than anything is not high-risk work with good controls. Because high-risk work with good controls isn't very risky.

What scares him is high-risk work with no controls.

An example of what scared him was forklifts because forklifts have high consequences for failure, but very few controls. That presence of control is the magic potion for leaders. That makes all the difference.

We need to identify our critical hazards. And that's really going to sound important. That's going to really be a big deal. He said to save you a lot of time, you will need to identify your critical hazards, but the people who are experts in knowing where your critical hazards are already work for you. You pay them, and they're your employees. They know where all the hazards exist.

What you really want to do is continue beyond the identification of critical hazards. What you really want to do is to couple controls to those hazards that you identify. So at the end of this project you don't end up with a list of things that will kill people.

You actually end up with a list of ways to control the energy from events that normally would kill people.

Golden rules tend to identify very specific behaviors, and we ask workers not to do those behaviors.

In reality, we want to assume workers will drift, assume workers will become complacent, assume workers will make mistakes, assume workers aren't perfect, and build a system around those workers that actually have the presence of control.

Now, to do that, I think we should change the golden rules to golden controls.

So instead of saying "don't fall", let's say "don't climb if you're not on scaffolding, or a ladder, or somehow controlled". It's tough because we've put much weight in morally managing workers to do the right thing. The assumption is that the worker's the problem. But workers don't die because they're the problem.

Workers die because there is no way to manage the energy between the worker and the hazard. We want to build a system that doesn't call the worker the problem. It actually says the worker is the solution. And the worker can manage controls around that risk more effectively than anybody else in the organization.

When you start looking at risk as not being the thing to control, it changes how you look at stop work. In fact, I would suggest that instead of asking workers to stop working, a much smarter thing would be to ask them, "when this job fails, what will kill you?" And they'll have an answer.

Then you ask them, "When that thing happens because we don't have perfect systems, don't have perfect people, don't have perfect processes, don't have perfect customers, don't have perfect conditions when the failure happens, what controls do we count on to not die?" Once they identify those controls, you ask them one other question, and this question from a senior leader is vital: Is that enough? Those controls we identified, are those sufficient?

And if your guys tell you "yeah, these controls are what work and this is enough", then you change from stop work authority to start work authority, and tell them "Okay, these three essential controls must be present every time we do this work. If one or three are not in place, we won't start the job until they are." And now you have put the onus for starting work on when you have certainty and clarity.

You can actually audit and manage and validate the presence of these controls. And you put the onus on starting the job when safe, not stopping the job when dangerous. If I were to send a senior leader into the field, I would have them go out and look for places where risky work is being done well, validate in that risky work the presence of controls, and then celebrate those controls as being effective and being used.

We should change golden rules to golden controls. Dr Todd Conklin.

CONTROLS SAVE LIVES - A PRINCIPLE, VALUE, MINDSET OR PRACTICE? - JEFFERY LYTH

Is the notion of "Controls Save Lives" a principle, value, mindset, or practice?

Before we explore that, it is useful to understand the differences between a principle, value, mindset, and practice, especially in the context of HOP, which can be crucial for applying these concepts effectively. Here's a breakdown:

Principle

Definition: A principle is a fundamental truth or proposition that serves as the foundation for a system of belief or behavior. Principles are guiding rules or laws that underpin a particular approach or philosophy.

In HOP: The five HOP principles are foundational ideas that guide how organizations should approach safety, risk management, and human performance. These principles are meant to influence and inform decisions and actions within the organization.

Value

Definition: A value is a deeply held belief or standard that guides behavior and decision-making. Values represent what is important to individuals or organizations.

In HOP: Values might influence how the principles are prioritized or interpreted. For example, if safety is a core value, it might drive an organization to adopt HOP principles more rigorously.

Mindset

Definition: A mindset is an established set of attitudes held by someone. It's the mental framework through which a person or organization views and approaches situations.

In HOP: A HOP mindset would involve viewing errors as opportunities for learning, understanding that variability is inherent in human performance, and the importance of building capacity. The mindset is about how you think, which influences how you apply them.

Practice

Definition: A practice is the actual application or use of an idea, belief, or method, as opposed to theories or ideas about them. It's what you do in your day-to-day operations.

In HOP: Practices are the specific actions or procedures that are implemented based on the HOP principles. For example, conducting Learning Teams to learn from incidents and improve future performance is a practice informed by HOP principles.

In summary

The HOP principles act as the "guiding philosophy" (**principles**) that inform the **mindset** of safety and risk management in an organization. This mindset is shaped by the organization's **values** and is reflected in the specific **practices** used to manage human performance and organizational processes.

Principles guide **why** you do things a certain way.

Values inform **what** is important in your approach.

Mindset influences **how** you think about applying the principles.

Practices are **what** you actually do to implement the principles and mindset in daily operations.

"CONTROLS SAVE LIVES" AS A PRINCIPLE

The principle "Controls Save Lives" aligns seamlessly with the core tenets of HOP, which emphasizes understanding and managing the complexities of human behavior in organizations. HOP acknowledges that human error is inevitable, and the system's resilience hinges on robust controls designed to manage these errors effectively.

In operations, the principle of "Controls Save Lives" is reflected in the iterative processes that allow teams to identify risks early and incorporate feedback loops to continuously improve safety controls. This emphasis on adaptability and responsiveness supports the HOP approach by ensuring that controls are not static but evolve as the work progresses, reflecting the latest understanding of risks and errors.

"CONTROLS SAVE LIVES" AS A VALUE

The value of "Controls Save Lives" is central to creating a culture of safety and resilience. In HOP, this value is tied to the recognition that controls are essential for managing the inherent variability in human performance including the workgroup commitment to delivering not just functional, but also safe and reliable products or services.

As a value, it also supports worker empowerment and trust. Workers must be empowered to engage with controls meaningfully. This value fosters an environment where team members feel responsible for safety and are trusted to make decisions that uphold this. This is visible with improved transparency and communication in the form of increased reporting and discussion of potential risks and control failures without fear of blame, promoting continuous learning and improvement.

"CONTROLS SAVE LIVES" AS A MINDSET

The mindset that "Controls Save Lives" is integral to HOP. This mindset is characterized by a continuous awareness of the role that controls play in mitigating risk and the importance of adaptability and responsiveness to new information. This is essential when workers are responding to and managing variability. In these situations, the mindset is not about rigidly adhering to a predefined plan but about adapting controls in response to emerging risks and changing circumstances. We set workers up for good work when the system and culture encourage teams to think ahead and plan for potential failures, making recovery smoother and more efficient.

Rather than "empowering" workers to **STOP** work when it becomes unsafe, we should encourage workers to **START** work when they believe it is safe and **PAUSE** to create space to understand the potential of variability when work changes and adjust their plan.

This supports a curious and continuous learning mindset, where understanding and improving controls are ongoing processes driven by the insights gained from both why work goes well and when it doesn't.

"CONTROLS SAVE LIVES" AS A PRACTICE

In practice, "Controls Save Lives" is operationalized through the day-to-day activities that ensure safety controls are;

■ implemented, monitored, and refined.

■ Are adequate and discuss what new controls might be needed as the project evolves.

In practice, this means embedding safety considerations into every aspect of work, from initial planning through to delivery. Active feedback loops are crucial for ensuring that controls remain relevant, effective, and continuously evaluated and updated.

HOP practices like the 4D's® encourage the use of feedback from frontline workers to refine controls, ensuring they are grounded in the realities of the work environment and are responsive to new information.

This aligns with HOP's focus on managing variability and adapting to changing conditions.

> The principle "Controls Save Lives" is not a rule to be followed but a comprehensive approach that permeates the organizational culture, mindset, and daily practices. By embedding this principle into every aspect of operations, organizations can create environments where safety is integral to success, ensuring that controls truly save lives.

The 6th Principal in Practice - Josh Bryant, Mitchell Services.

I'd been trained in the five HOP principles in early 2018, and they resonated with me at a personal level because these principles were heavily aligned with my own values and beliefs. I recognized the need to be better at practicing the 'Leaders Response Matters' principle and role-modeling this to others in our leadership teams. We continued implementing the principles within the business, mainly focusing on leader knowledge of the principles, our investigations, and communication of events, and then a slow move into operational learning.

I saw Todd Conklin live in July 2019, and it was in that session that he raised the idea of the sixth principle—'Controls Save Lives.' It made me go back and read his book, 'Workplace Fatalities—A Failure to Predict.' This highlighted again that fatalities are always based upon uncontrolled energy and that serious events live in successful/normal work.

There was a major methane fire in an underground mine where we operated, and this led to the mining industry being called out for better fatal risk management (Critical Risks) and the implementation of critical controls. We completed this assessment and implementation of critical control standards and verifications relatively quickly.

But how do we make this meaningful to our workforce, particularly leaders?

This is where we added 'Controls Saves Lives' to our HOP Principles—because this principle reinforced and supported the other principles but also kept the idea of risk alive. It also reinforced that this critical control work was important and fundamental to operational excellence.

I've sometimes felt a bit guilty having this as a sixth principle – like I'm not a 'HOP purest' and changed things to suit. I've also had discussions with some of the HOP Pioneers who have told me that the idea of controls is built into the other principles. In my context, this principle is used in practice to understand the degradation of controls, ease of use of controls, risk important actions and critical steps for what must always go right, and those mitigating controls that give us the ability to fail safely.

For us, the principle of 'controls save lives' has been supported by the other principles and has now become how we do business. - Josh Bryant

CHAPTER TWO: SEEING CRITICAL CONTROLS IN PRACTICE

WAYS TO APPLY THE PRINCIPLES

Applying the 5 Principles of HOP in practice involves a shift in thinking and approach to safety and reliability in the workplace. Here's how you can apply each principle:

■ **Error is normal. Even the best people make mistakes.** Recognize that errors are a part of human nature and build systems that anticipate and mitigate these errors so that "people can fail safely" or "the system can fail gracefully" in managing the presence or transfer of energy from the event that could cause harm.

■ **Context influences behavior. Systems drive outcomes.** Understand that the work environment and systems in place heavily influence employee behavior. Regularly review and improve these systems to ensure they promote and allow safe behavior.

■ **Blame fixes nothing.** Instead of blaming individuals for errors, focus on understanding why the error occurred and how the system allowed it. This involves fostering a culture of open communication and learning, where employees feel safe to report errors and near misses.

■ **How you respond to failure matters. How leaders act and respond counts.** Leaders should respond to failures in a way that promotes learning and improvement rather than blame. This could involve conducting thorough incident investigations to understand how the failure occurred and how to prevent it in the future rather than punishing individuals for errors. Moving from "**who failed**" (the person) to "**what failed**" (the system).

■ **Learning and Improving is vital. Learning is deliberate.** Encourage continuous learning and improvement. This could involve regular training sessions, learning from everyday work in the field, near misses and incidents, and constantly seeking ways to improve safety protocols and work design.

Remember, these principles should guide the development, implementation, and improvement of your safety systems, procedures, worker engagement, and the overall safety culture of the organization.

They should be communicated and discussed to all workers and ingrained in the organization's culture as **"how we do things around here"** commitment and ownership by leadership.

HOP ACTIVITY

INTRODUCTION

In this activity, we are looking for the value of applying the practice of Controls Save Lives.

And for you to reflect on those engagements and conversations with people. This is also an excellent opportunity to have a leader or colleague you work with or someone you see as a coach or mentor "**learning buddy**." Your role is to undertake the activity and then reflect. The other person's role is to listen, reflect, and provide observations on the HOP principles.

The five principles of HOP are:

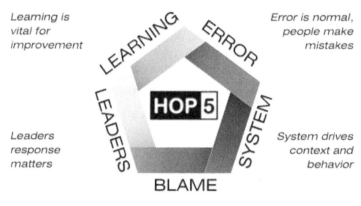

Learning is vital for improvement

Error is normal, people make mistakes

Leaders response matters

System drives context and behavior

Blame fixes nothing

The HOP 5 Pentagon © Learning Teams Inc, 2024.

THINKING ABOUT YOUR JOURNEY OF LEARNING

During the exercise, there will be places to write. Think of this as a way to reflect on your learning journey. Your writing should not be a purely descriptive account of what you did and learned. It is an opportunity to communicate your thinking process about:

- How and why did you do what you did?
- What do you now think about what you did?
- What you can do differently next time?

When we reflect, we are more likely to develop a deeper understanding of ourselves, how we learn, and what we need to do to gain further skills. When we apply reflective practice, we are:

- More motivated as we know what we are trying to achieve and why.
- We can use our existing knowledge to help us develop our understanding of new ideas.
- Understand new concepts by relating them to our previous experiences.
- Develop our learning and thinking by building on the critical evaluation of our prior learning experiences.
- More self-aware and able to identify, explain, and address their strengths and weaknesses.

"Self-reflection is a humbling process. It's essential to find out why you think, say, and do certain things – then better yourself." – Sonya Teclai"

APPLYING PRACTICE

Think of a job, task, or activity that people do in your organization that has a hazard that could cause life-changing or life-altering harm. Ideally, two or more people perform this job, task, or activity, and the hazard has critical controls (things that manage energy), critical steps (things that influence people), and a life-saving, critical, or cardinal rule linked to it. In many organizations, these rules remind workers of the measures they should or shouldn't take to protect their own safety. They draw attention to the activities most likely to lead to a fatality and the life-saving actions an individual controls. Examples of such rules are:

- Exclusion zones (e.g., when lifting operations occur or to separate workers from mobile plant and equipment)

- Energy Isolation (e.g., the use of lock out - tag out procedures)

- Working At Height (e.g., blanket height limit or use of fall arrest system)

- Do not exceed speed limits

- Keep clear of danger zones on machinery (e.g., nip points, crush zones)

Ask that small group of people (2 to 5) that you want to learn more about what they do by asking questions and listening to their stories about everyday work. Make sure they know that you are doing this as a learning exercise, and feel free to share with them about HOP and the five principles; it will help to make them curious. Remember, this is more than asking as many questions as possible or trying to learn about everything they do. The group will respond to you once they see that they are being listened to, respected, able to share stories, encouraged to participate, and recognized as experts in their work. And please remember;

"The greatest enemy to learning is knowing." – John C. Maxwell

PART ONE: LEARNING QUESTIONS FROM THE WORKGROUP

Write down the job, task, or activity you are learning about.

Write down the "Critical Risks" that have been identified in the job, task, or activity.

Write down the "Critical Controls" to manage the Critical Risks.

Write down the "Life-saving or Cardinal rules" that workers must rely on.

Question: When doing that work, what is the hazard (STKY - Stuff That Can Kill You), and what is the energy type (energy wheel[3]) of the hazard?

---

[3] https://www.safetyfunction.com/energy-based-safety

Question: What controls that manage energy do you rely on to stay safe?

Question: What steps, methods, or rules do you rely on to stay safe?

Question: When applying the "life-saving rule" to do your work safely, do you have to?

Rule Option	Yes or No
Change the work to comply with the rule	
Change the rules to get the work done	
Make new rules to get the work done	
Not use the rules to get the work done	

Question: When applying the "life-saving rule" to do your work safely, has the rule worked in every scenario so far?

Question: How accessible, doable, and relatable are your procedures?

Question: What do you do to make the job easier?

Question: Can you share a story when something didn't go as planned, and you believe it could have gone wrong or did go wrong?

PART TWO: YOUR REFLECTION

Write down your learnings and reflections on the stories shared by the group against the HOP principles.

Write: Your thoughts about how error is normal and how even the best people can make mistakes.

Write: Your thoughts about whether the system and rules are designed to support "good and successful" work.

Write: What are your thoughts about how the context of workers sharing their stories was evidenced in their behavior with you?

Write: What are your thoughts about how the organization sees successful work compared to the workers who do the work and face the risk every day?

PART THREE: SHARING AND FEEDBACK WITH OTHERS

Take the opportunity to share your Part One: Learning Questions and Part Two: Reflections with your learning buddy.

Question: What did you learn from this activity?

Question: What did your learning buddy take from this activity?

Question: Discuss and record with your learning buddy how you could take this learning and apply it in a small way in your work each day.

Question: Discuss and record with your learning buddy what other opportunities you could find to share your learnings with others.

ADDITIONAL RESOURCES

You can download PDF versions of Parts One, Two, and Three at:

https://hoptool.com/46ZTZcV or scan the QR code below.

This is the beginning of your journey, and you can't go out and fix everything. Creating sustainable change happens in small increments.

CHAPTER THREE: REFLECT ON YOUR LEARNINGS

MY THOUGHTS MOVING FORWARD - BRENT SUTTON

One of the risks associated with introducing "Controls Save Lives" as a formal principle is that it may be perceived as just another slogan or safety campaign. The history of safety management is replete with well-intentioned initiatives that, over time, become diluted into mere checklists or compliance exercises. Campaigns like "Zero Harm," while aspirational, have often been criticized for creating unrealistic expectations and inadvertently shifting the focus from learning and improvement to achieving an unattainable goal.

The 6th principle is at risk of falling into a similar trap if it is not implemented with a deep understanding of its underlying intent. If organizations treat "Controls Save Lives" as a simple directive to be enforced rather than a complex and adaptive approach to managing risk, it could lead to a superficial application of the principle. This could result in a culture where the presence of controls is checked off as a procedural requirement rather than being critically assessed and continuously improved.

To avoid the pitfalls associated with safety campaigns, it is crucial that the 6th principle is embedded into the organizational culture in a way that promotes continuous learning and adaptation. This requires a shift in mindset from seeing controls as static barriers to viewing them as dynamic components of a resilient safety system.

One way to achieve this is by ensuring that the principle is not treated as an end in itself but as part of an ongoing conversation about safety and risk management. Leaders should encourage open dialogue about the effectiveness of controls, inviting feedback from workers on the frontline who interact with these controls daily. This approach aligns with the broader HOP philosophy, which values the insights of workers and sees them as critical to understanding and managing risks.

Additionally, organizations must resist the temptation to quantify or measure the success of "Controls Save Lives" in the same way that traditional safety campaigns are often measured. For example, rather than setting targets for the number of controls implemented, the focus should be on the quality and effectiveness of those controls. This means regularly reviewing and adapting controls based on new information, changing conditions, and lessons learned from incidents.

The principle should be seen as a tool for fostering a culture of curiosity and continuous improvement rather than as a set of rules to be rigidly followed. This can be supported through practices like 4D's®, 4L's®, and Learning Teams, where workers and leaders come together to explore how work is done, what controls are in place, and how these controls can be improved. By focusing on the real-world application of controls and learning from both successes and failures, the 6th principle can be integrated into the fabric of the organization in a meaningful way.

Leadership plays a crucial role in ensuring that the 6th principle does not become just another safety campaign. Think about how leaders can model the behaviors and attitudes that support a nuanced understanding of controls and their role in safety management.

Examples of this include being curious and genuinely interested in how controls are applied in the field, validating their effectiveness, and being open to making changes when necessary.

Leaders should also be wary of framing the principle in absolutes. The reality is that no control is perfect, and no system is entirely free of risk. By acknowledging this complexity, leaders can foster a culture where controls are seen as part of a broader strategy to manage risk rather than as fail-proof solutions.

The organization should embed the principle into its culture as part of an ongoing process of learning and adaptation. This requires a shift away from the campaign mentality that has characterized many safety initiatives in the past and towards a more holistic approach that values continuous improvement and the insights of workers on the frontline.

By fostering open dialogue and learning, the 6th principle can achieve its intended impact: not just as a slogan but as a critical component of a resilient safety system that truly saves lives.

THE AUTHORS

Brent Sutton

Brent is well regarded as a safety coach and for taking organizations on a learning journey to understand how people are seen as the solution, how to engage people and leverage their skills so that worker participation becomes a normal way of running an organization where everybody benefits. Brent is the co-author of the best selling books on Learning Teams, Learning From Everyday Work, The 4Ds for HOP and Learning Teams, and host of the podcast show "The Practice of Learning Teams" and "HOP Into Action". He resides in Auckland, New Zealand.

Jeffery Lyth

Jeff is a well regarded innovator in workplace safety leadership. He helps organizations evolve how they manage safety by guiding their exploration and integration of the 'new view' of safety principles and helping them break through the performance plateaus associated with conventional views of health and safety and the owner of www.safetydifferently.com.

Jeff is the co-author of the best selling books on Learning From Everyday Work, The 4Ds for HOP and Learning Teams. He resides in North Vancouver, British Columbia, Canada.

Made in United States
Orlando, FL
18 September 2024

51687730R00039